THROUGH THE WINDOW

A COLLECTION OF POEMS

by

J. R. Ashley

Published by

MELROSE BOOKS

An Imprint of Melrose Press Limited
St Thomas Place, Ely
Cambridgeshire
CB7 4GG, UK
www.melrosebooks.com

FIRST EDITION

Cover designed by Nikki Bovis-Coulter

ISBN 978 1 906050 04 7

Printed and bound in Great Britain by:
CPI Antony Rowe, Bumpers Farm, Chippenham,
Wiltshire, SN14 6LH, UK

POEMS ALREADY PUBLISHED

Winter Sheep	*That's Life!*
The Wig	*That's Life!*
Blindness	*The Coventry Poetry Prize 1999, Millennium Anthology*
The Loner (now called "The Lost Gem")	*Countryside Tales*
Waste	*Countryside Tales*
Spring	*Countryside Tales*
Autumn	*Countryside Tales*
It	*United Press Ltd*

CONTENTS

Truth at best is but an honest opinion
at any point in time:
it is illusory to think it is absolute.

ACKNOWLEDGEMENTS

I would like to thank my two friends
Alan Taylor and Jim Worrall
without whose help and patience
I would not have been able to proceed.
All characters mentioned in the text are imaginary
and bare no relation to anyone living

DANCE WITH THE ORANGES

Dance, dance
So long as you are able,
Dance with the oranges
At the Captain's table.

Dance, dance
Whilst things are stable,
Dance with the oranges
At the Captain's table.

Dance till the decks begin to strain,
Dance till the engines stall,
Dance till the lights flick out
And the sirens call.

Dance till the oranges are dark and salty
Bobbing on the waves in the night
Where the sea and oceans meet
Above the wreckage site.

Dance, dance,
Dance with the oranges,
Dance till the last of the juice has drained,
Dance till the pith has gone
And there is nothing left
To dance upon.

THIS MOMENT

This moment stands tall,
A pillar reaching high,
The unfettered wherewithal;
But quickly it is cluttered
With bones of yesterday,
And wallows
In vacillation about tomorrow,
Till it can only point
A tentative finger
Towards its aspiration.

Why, when it is obvious,
Is it difficult to see
That now is the only time
That can be certain,
And can reach its potential
To influence the way of things?

WINTER SHEEP

When flurries in a hurry
Turn to heavy falls of snow
And the poor four-legged creatures
Have nowhere else to go,
They stand and stare and are blinded
And are in a different stew,
From the one they were predestined
To be in for me and you!

ASPIRATION

There is a song
That simply sings
The whole day long
And is never heard.

There is a light
That lingers long,
That glows
But never shows.

Will one day
That light lift high
And with a song
Illuminate the sky?

MINNEHAHA

I found a cup of laughing water
And although I knew I shouldn't oughter
I gave it to my ailing daughter.

First a fit of giggles hectic,
Next her stomach wiggled peptic
Then completely apoplectic.

The doctor from his bag he took
A needle with a fishing hook.
He made an incision,
Unhooked the collision
And went on his way cock-a-hoop.

Now Minnie with her laughing waters,
Tucked up tight in her private quarters,
Dreams all day without a bother
Of her beloved, Hiawatha.

GLIMPSE OF CLEAR WATER

It comes slow into the garden,
Low in the mud,
And tangles in the rhizomes
Of wild water iris.

It stops at the weir,
Clears as it settles
Before inching over
Into the sunlight
Breaking its silence
Into chinks of laughing diamonds.

It has no capacity to wait,
To sate the appetite of casual witness,
And quick like a moment's fun
Is gone.

LOVE LETTERS

Bring them all together,
Tie them up with string,
Put them in a plastic bag
And give them their last fling.

Over the hedge
And over the towpath
(The dirty, filthy fibber)
Over the wet, uncomfortable stones
Into the river.

But nay I put them back
With lavender and with lace.
Perhaps one day he will come back
And we'll again embrace.

WILD GEESE

The flying machine
Spreads across the sky
Breaking the silence.

Up and over the pylon wires
This great machine
Synchronises its flexibility.

Skimming the trees,
Lowering to the lake
It disintegrates.

Pieces white and grey fragment
Which flap and bark
And assume again their individuality.

The golden evening
Resumes its stillness,
Its sky a cornfield reaped.

BLINDNESS (1)

Gone are the lights and colour
And movement;
Pictures,
Written words.

There is now a broad expanse
Waiting to be filled;
A plain white blankness
On which to weave
Innumerable imaginings.

Shapes
Cut by sounds and thought
Stretch and taste
And fill the nostrils with rich spices.
Faint murmurings splash,
And whispers
Add subtle symbols of harmony.

But then a wipeout.
Venom surges
Where imagination has strayed,
And the ego
Grasps at anger
And demands without gratitude
The helping hand
As if it were a slave.
Spaces fill with bitterness
And ooze self-pity,
And black clouds brood.

Slowly comes the reluctant dawn,
Hesitates on the horizon
Then its thin band spreads a new reality
And the world becomes a small
And yet bigger place.

THE LOST GEM

Everything is still,
Too cold for birds to fly,
Even the thrill
Of shivering to get by
Is frozen.

It is as if
The world has touched its peak,
The will to lift,
To reach, to leap
Is broken.

Later when the sun comes out
And the air is warm,
Everything will turn about
And be reborn;
The past will be forgotten.

But something somewhere will have gone,
Something simple lost
That before had shone
Like a single star.

WASTE

He leans in the hollows
Of the evening sun,
Soon to be gone
Leaving no signpost to follow,
Only a shadow to think upon.

He leaves the same familiar field to plough,
The same banks and pits and undulations;
He leaves us to begin where he began,
Same problems and frustrations.

If only we were born
With the wisdom of the soul departed;
Not with the innocence of the womb
And a meaningless tomb!

THE TIDE

Isn't it odd
To feel that God
Is not on your side,
To be alone,
Prone to be someone
Other than whom you thought,
Fraught with uncertainty
In calm waters,
Thinking to be inviolate
Yet so vulnerable
That worms
Eat you away
In the small hours?

But in the morning,
Seeing
The old shipwreck
Lying in the sand
With its nose upturned
Into the ruck of rocks,
One senses
How soon the tide will turn
And the disaster be swamped
With the smooth murmurings
Of the sea,
Burying the wreck
And the memory.

And seagulls will reappear
And God's battered world
Will swirl
With the freshness
Of new day.

How odd of God!

THE INTELLECTUAL

Frenetic eyes
Look down beneath the claustrophobic sea
To reach the sky
And failing
Turn but inward to the rat-infested shore.

Why do these eyes
That draw
Peculiar sketches on an ordinary face
And imaginings on the real world,
Why do they see
Everything so wildly complex
That happiness is sorrow
That there is only tomorrow,
When time itself is infinite
And simplicity is the depth of all understanding?

SIMON

In the beginning,
In the yard at school
Thunderstruck
And screwed into his mind
A clock that had stopped.

The germ of creation,
The promise of enlightenment
In the first step he had taken
Were swallowed in that one moment
And his intended self
Vanished.

Parts of him became crippled
And before their time
Twisted like the old oak
That stood forever on the hill.

The parts that were left
Stayed ludicrously innocent,
Unmarked, untouched,
Untouchable;
His simple words and imagination
Painted the uncomplicated scene
Of what he was now
And what we had all squandered
In our gallop into manhood.

ROMAN VILLA

Echoes of a town
Fallen down
Under the gentle ghostly hammer
Of two millennia.

Humans animated once
This scarred domain.
Craftsman's sweat and pain
Carved the symmetry,
The pillars, the bold facade
Designed by scholars, statesmen,
Now interred
In nature's backdrop.

They could be retrieved,
They could again be seen
If the two extremes,
Then and Now,
Stood apart from their smothering in-between.

For evolution spreads
Its glutinous web
Like mountain mists
And shrouds distinctive peaks
With mediocrity
And fills the valleys
With the dross of passing time.

MEMORY

When we remember,
How does it show itself,
In what configuration?

Does it come
In familiar shape,
In light, in darkness,
In black, in white,
In colour, in sepia?

What is it of a tree we see
When it isn't there,
Visible in its invisibility,
Pervasively a part
Of what had been determined?

Does memory come
In the perfume of a summer night,
The turn of a familiar page,
At the sight of the pond
With the trailing willow
And the sun tracking through?

Does it come
At a least-expected moment
Putting perspective into a weary day
When its manifestation
Without sound or shape or substance
Is more real than anything else?

SUNSET DAYS

Together we are here in the doldrums
Sitting close up to the wall;
Three feet apart we are and staring
Waiting for no one to call.

The table in the middle beckons
But it's out of reach in no-man's-land;
In Victorian days this was the parlour
Now stale urine and aerosol cans.

Can anyone think that once we were normal beings,
Had mothers and sisters and brothers,
That we held aloft our self-respect,
That we even had our lovers?

Dear God, there surely must be something more
That you can bring about
Than to lead us to this cabbage patch
And drop us out.

MOUNTAIN LAKE

The lake lies flat
Like a mirror in a wooded frame
Reflecting the mountains, the trees,
And a sky, more blue
Than the sky itself.
A damsel fly,
Hovering in the sun,
Courts with vanity
Its own image.

The eagle,
Blind to all but her own thoughts,
Searches the washed-up debris
And the shallows at the water's edge;
She is still hurting
In bereavement.

All day she sits
Angrily bewildered,
The noise of the earlier storm
And her missing brood
Still bearing down upon her.
Then, without warning
She lifts up over the mountain
To seek solace
In the lonely peaks.

NEED!

Who indeed
Can identify need?
Ingenious politicians try
But satisfy
Only their self-esteem.

Need is a tempting word
Lured
By pontification,
By classification;
But the bureaucratic tongue
Is too cumbersome, too long.
It stumbles over income and cost,
Is lost
Between legitimate expense
And extravagance;
It cannot distinguish sloth
And worse
Is fooled by an empty purse.

How long does it take to see
That when help comes free
We are all in need,
That from this seed
Grows only greed?

HIATUS

Thin the shape of sound
In the aftermath of winter,
On the waterlogged path,
On the lawn lethargic with moss.

Thin the shape of sound
And quieter still
The bare earth
In the abandoned fields,
In the woods
Where no one comes,
Where the peat-pitched pond
Reeks with silence.

Thin the shape of sound
Where time between seasons
Belongs to no one.

LIGHT CRAFT

Over the lucid lake
The light craft glides
To aspiration at the other side:
An easy task
For self-congratulation.

But if overhead
Appears a cloud
And wind is loud,
Determination
Slips away.

If squalls erupt
And slants of rain
Obliquely stain
The canvas sail,
Cries and wails
As crewmen panic
Like scudding rats
On the doomed *Titanic.*

CUCKOO IN THE NEST

There is an integration
Of the artist and his patron
With his public, with his critic,
With his friends.
But into this congregation
As if by incubation – a trespasser descends.

Down from the rafters
He seems to come
Or drips from the chandelier
Or squeezes through the crack in the wall
(One never sees him arrive at all)
And rarely is he a she, this entity.

He sidles and glides,
He strides the right stride,
He chooses his moment to speak.
He picks out his phrases
From textbook and praises
In English, in Latin, in Greek.

He is so more poetic,
More subtly aesthetic
Than Milton or Shakespeare or Keats;
The arias of Verdi
In Italian can barely
Keep up with his manner of speech.

He floats at a distance
From oil paintings to pastels,
His hands now expressing finesse;
Enchantment of Manet,
Picasso and Monet
He finds he can hardly repress.

The small congregation
Is in mild agitation
When he departs for a soirée elsewhere,
But before they can breathe
Corporate sighs of relief
His twin comes in from thin air.

ROOFSCAPE

(From a high back-window of a shopping street in Buxton)

Lean roofs,
Red roofs,
Roofs of aluminium;
Slate roofs, tile roofs
Elite and for the minions,
High roofs, low roofs
New and antique,
Flat roofs and Georgian
And roofs that leak.

All inaccessible,
No one can see them
Except from this window,
With no ground between them.

Here one thrills
At being alone,
At life suspended,
Where no one interferes with time
And no roofs are mended.

HOLIDAYS

Palm trees and sand,
Seas rippled with warm jewels;
We call this blissful overwash
A time for renewal.

Touring foreign lands,
Snapping pictures of the Sphinx,
Grecian amphitheatres, Roman roads,
Spanish vistas and fizzy drinks.

Climbing, walking different paths,
Remote peaks and precious finds;
Are these the new horizons
Refreshing our exhausted minds?

Is there a reek sometimes of conscience,
Some nibbling demon asks,
Putting off today and tomorrow
Back home some difficult task?

Does it signify bituminous coverings
Of personal worrisome cares
That will appear again like holes in the road
When the surface wears?

POEM

There is a poem
Lurking in the stream,
Sometimes sombre, sometimes bright,
Trying for a moment
To walk the bank,
Then plunging out of sight
As if exposure would destroy
Its very soul.

VILLAGE CHURCH

On weekdays,
Unhindered dusty shafts of sunlight
Slant across the chancel steps.

On Sundays,
Camphorated coats and hats, and organ sounds
Perforate the vacuum.

Through it all,
Through dust and rain and congregation,
The building stands immense.

The one immortal symbol,
Like the air we breathe
And leave behind.

TEA AND CAKES

A great sheet of rain
Falls this side of the tall trees,
Intruding upon our patch,
Introducing vagaries and storm clouds
To complacent lives.

Something we cannot stop
Drags away the elegant dust
Of sweet content,
And challenges our normality,
Threatens our ten o'clock tea and cakes.

Why should this satisfaction be swept aside
When it has slowly and patiently
Become part of us?
Who wants innovation, excitement and challenge
When wisdom oozes slow,
And drips upon familiar things?

OUTPATIENTS

We are tall and thin
In long, narrow passages,
On small, uncomfortable chairs.

We line the walls
Like nondescript wallpaper,
Eyes searching the antiseptic floor
Because there is nothing else.

Day hangs long
Endlessly stretching artificial light
Into continuous tedium.

We had heard
Of nurses being understaffed;
Here they stand and stare,
Relieve the boredom
By marching up and down,
Orbiting our outer flanks
With sharp, sheepdog-wary eyes.

They count us:
Thirteen, fourteen
Twenty-one, twenty-two;
They shuffle our records
And probably get us out of turn.

We are cattle
In trucks at the dockside;
Empty cartons
Littering the walkways;
Atomic waste
Trapped in vitreous slabs.

Perhaps in an hour
The consultant will arrive;
More likely, his understudy
With hope in his heart
That he will inherit the kingdom.

We wait, we wait,
We continue to wait,
Convincing ourselves
That perhaps there is something better
On the other side.

TWO LEAVES

Stuck on the road
In the autumn rain
The fallen leaf
Is worn away.

Identical twin
Blown by the wind
To the garden shed
Has come to stay.

FARM KITCHEN

Windows open to the orchard
And close by
Clustered cotoneaster blossom
Clings precariously like lean snow
To a hanging gate.

Inside
The tired clop
Of heavy boots on stone floor
Echoes the hollowness
Of the cellar beneath.

Over the mantle,
Prime on the wall,
Lit by the full sun
Hangs the masterpiece
Fruit on a Georgian Table.

In the corner
The now decrepit table
Is shrouded in dust,
The bowl is cracked,
The fruit long gone.

Herein, the tale of six generations
Moving through to the dawn
Of a new millennium.

THOUGHT FOR FOOD

Let the deli ducks all dangle
In the food shops in The Dingle
Whilst the rich folks loudly jangle
Their jewels and their bangles.

Give me instead by far
The smell of vinegar
And let a portion pass my lips
Of unwrapped fish and chips.

STING

Life is as it is – a pretence,
A selfish contradiction so intense;
It fills its ego, its every move
With evidence to prove
Its true regard for other people,
But whilst so doing, trickles its treacle
Sweet and sticky, an attractive bed
In which to spin its spider's web.

INSIDE OUT

When you wake up in the morning
And it's night instead of day,
And the frolic moon is dancing
On the river and the hay,
When summer should be winter
With frost hard on the ground,
But the grass is just like tinder
And there's rose scent all around,
And the temperature is breeding gnats
When it's just about year end,
Then you wonder if the world is flat
And you are round the bend.

THE LUNCHEON CLUB

"Oh, put it in the back lane, please!"
Said the landlord of the Cheshire Cheese.
So I took my van, I had no choice,
From the car park next to the black Rolls Royce.

Back in the pub I ordered a cider;
He offered a half if I made no moither,
And would I drink it in the tap room where
No one came and wouldn't stare.

A bag of crisps I then asked for.
"Crisps!" he yelled, "That's the last straw."
He fell to the ground, in a fit epileptic;
The village inn, I quickly left it.

JUDGEMENT

So simple – black or white;
But might the wings
Of everyday things
Rest between
The two extremes,
Fall
Where Mother Teresa's shawl
And the deeds of Cromwell Street
Meet?

BEATRICE

Is it cursed
This empty road where no one comes,
Where an unsuspecting dog
Halts, sniffs and turns away,
Where trees
Form a canopy
Yet there are no birds?

But then it comes –
A voice laughing,
Laughing like a stream
Starting in the mountains,
Fresh and vibrant
Throwing crystal waters
Into the baseness of the late afternoon.

Light and clarity
Spread and absorb the protracted void,
The cursed empty road
Suddenly fills with voices singing,
With the rhythm of dancing feet,
With colours merging:
The loneliness has gone.

SCENT

Scent has looks
And has shape
That footsteps follow.

If it were betrayed
Its colour would fade;
But its looks and shape
Are there forever.

If it moves
It will not die,
But will gather instead
More subtle perfume.

And new footsteps will follow.

WIND

Where does the wind come from,
Where does it go,
Seeming to think only to arrive
And move on?

Sowing as it reaps
It heaps
Untimely debris
In neat corners.

And like man to the end
Whose mortality rests
In a handful of dust
It wears itself out.

SOPHIE

I met a man at ten o'clock
Who said his wife had run amok.
We had a drink till half past three
And then we had a cream cake tea,
But when we heard she'd done her face in
We really had a celebration.

THE WIG

He wouldn't buy it,
He gave me no option
But to take it to
The antique auction.

And there the bidding started low
But then two experts in the know
Lifted it up to an excellent price
They'd found it full of antique lice!

APPLE ORCHARD

That night beneath the open stars
And poppied blooms of apple blossom
Clinging tight against the fitful wind,
That night when shackles were loosened
And I was free to search in realms,
Till then another world
Hovering by in mist and fantasy . . .

That night
Wisdom and reason combined,
Their tentacles entwined
Into strands of compatibility,
And together they pointed out and inwards
Through sociability and lonesomeness
To the comprehensive oneness of the soul.

That night life shone clear like a silhouette
Black against a backcloth of ivory,
But the night moved on.
Pale beckoning dawn
Brought frost to the apple blossom.

BORDER COUNTRY

The weeds
In the castle field
Dare to steal up
Over the moat
To the ruined walls
And beyond.

In retaliation
The blinding rain
From mid Wales
Pelts down its arrows
From its quiver in the clouds.

The mountain stream
Knowing no boundary,
And the wind
Seething amongst the sparse trees
Act as dual and only witness.

The ancient war goes on
Fierce and unremitting
With a purpose
That needs some understanding.

The human being
Seems far removed
But for the ghostly strain,
Best left unheard,
Of an unborn infant crying.

DANCE

The wind sweeps up
Over the rocks and cliffs from the sea,
Lifts and folds in undulations on the hills,
Dissipates amongst the scree,
Then comes and goes with no identity
Amongst the clouds of an English summer sky.

Commingle it, still in England,
With the blast and cold of winter,
The sharp stimulations of spring,
The heavy, damp hangings of autumn.

Contrast it
With the dry, hot gusts of the Kalahari
The warm Sirocco,
The Mistral sweeping down to the Mediterranean,
The frantic tortured halos
Severing the Himalayas
From the rest of the world.

Bare them all
To a mind equally and contrarily
At peace and in passion,
Mercurially, everlastingly in change;
Then take them as a partner,
And dance.

EARTH

Earth is the object
Towards which
Everything is drawn,
And of which
Everything becomes a part.

Earth witnesses our conception,
Watches us grow
And become our own being:
Human, fish, beast, bird,
Flower of the field
Or woodland tree
Searching out its personality.

Earth
Sees us mature,
Raise others in our likeness,
Grow old and die,
And give back
That which in life
We had taken away.

THE TEST

Wait,
You will see
What you wouldn't see
If you went away.

Wait,
If you go
You will inevitably wish
You had stayed.

Wait,
Wait and ponder,
Think
Before you wander off.

Wait,
Go only if you fear
That people will wonder
What you are at.

And if you do fear,
Go,
Go fast
And don't come back.

TOMORROW

Tomorrow is what tomorrow brings,
Tears and things
Or sunshine to a shady brook.

Tomorrow is an aching heart
As trains depart
Or fragrance at meetings in memorable places.

Tomorrow is what tomorrow brings,
Pressed between angel wings
That fly to new beginnings.

Tomorrow is what tomorrow brings,
Unpredictable daubings
Across today.

BUGS

Little twitches
Stitching itches
In places inaccessible,
So once again
Scratching is impossible.

If I could stretch my fingers
A little more
I'd stop wearing out
The corners of the door.

THE DANCING CLASS

Cream teas
Then a fun-run race for mothers
Across the village green,
For it is three fifteen;
The school bell rings
And infants burst through the yard
Out the gate into waiting arms.

Except Elsie;
She dawdles, wishing she wasn't there,
For no one waits for her.
Even the duck pond
Tucks itself up at the corners
And pretends to sleep,
Trying not to notice.

Soon she is alone.
Each day it is the same,
And people don't see her.
But if they do, they think,
"How odd,
How can anyone
Leave a child alone like this!"

Then they hug their precious jewels
And hurry them round the corner
To the dancing class.

THE VOICE

The solo voice comes up
From the body of the choir,
Like a tall tree rising from the rest,
Whose roots lie hidden
In the tangle on the forest floor.
When it stops
And the children break out of church,
And laugh and skip and hop
And dissipate their energies,
Not one stands out from all the rest,
Exemplifying the modesty,
The collective isolation,
Of the village that lies deep
In the folds of Pembroke Hill.

C. of E.

Parson Roberts,
Welsh though he be,
Is Church of England
Like you and me.

But his voice like dry bread
Turns up at the edges,
And he sings instead
Of saying his pledges.

And when he naively gazes down
At half-empty pews
And sees his congregation
Decidedly few.

It dawns very slowly
That we Church of E.
Attend only funerals
Regularly.

THE WATERING

Rain promises;
Thunder and lightning
And dark clouds
Crowd in;
A sudden high wind
Rips into summer leaves
Then whips up dust
From the wasteland,
But still no rain.

Instead it retreats;
A break in the clouds,
A chink of sunlight,
A rainbow boring into the hillside,
A patch of blue,
Then more.
There is stillness
And the sun digs down
Into everything.

Last vestiges of moisture
Evaporate from the pond,
And the wagtail
Flips across the dry waterfall
To seek out an isolated trickle
From amongst the overhanging ferns;
But there is none.
Flowers in pots and beds
Droop and wait.

They ask me to act as God
And in so doing
I miss
The evening six o'clock news and sport.

MUSIC

Does he exist,
He who has no music
In his soul?

Does he breathe,
He whose lungs
Are wracked with holes?

Does he move,
He whose limbs
No movement show?

Or see,
He whose eyes
Are forever closed?

No –
He does not exist,
He who has no music
In his soul!

THE UNCERTAINTY

I cannot ask it
To wait until the morning,
For it would be like
Holding back the sea:
I cannot contain it,
Its timing, its structure,
Or influence its promise of bright prospect
Or threat of darkness,
For it comes as a stranger.

It comes with no warning,
Touching, intruding, integrating;
It is to the mind
An ingestion of sustenance
As is food to the body,
And together, both body and mind combine
The visible with the invisible,
Into the enigma
That is life.

During my living
I witness another's death,
A body being stripped of all animation,
Its cupboards laid bare ready for burial
Deep in the dark earth.

What then of the mind,
The build-up of thought
Into a lifetime's knowledge?
Is that vanquished too,
Thus completing the cycle of man's existence?

Or does it reposition in another place
Where it can pause awhile,
To reflect on its experience,
Before moving on?

THE FORGET-ME-NOT

A pleadingly appropriate name,
Hidden in grass on the river bank,
In woods,
In extraordinary places in gardens,
Where the wind has carried its seed
Amongst the weeds.

It flowers within days
And is gone
Before the frontiers of summer come.
A runner,
A something slight in spring,
Less substantial than the primrose,
Not so lasting
Or casting throws of colour
As the bluebells do,
Amongst the trees and anemones.

Remembered immemorially
On Victorian jewellery
By its symbol of true love.
It is delicate, sensitive, shy
And points the way
To reasons why
Modesty will forever be
Fine of quality.

SPRING FROST

Grisly iron fist
Disguised in diamonds
Grips the fruit just set,
And turns potential
Into newborn death.

VIGNETTES

1. WINTER

Winter is strait-laced:
She is cruel to those who skip the truth,
For there is nowhere to hide.
The sun during the day,
The moon at night
Give light
That shows the flaws,
The blemishes of everyday.
The hill is plainly a hill,
The field is square,
The garden has no secrets,
No succulent growth
To dump the refuse behind;
Everywhere is black and white,
Open to be examined
And to be accounted for.

2. SPRING

Spring is a fairy prancing about:
Fizzy as a bottle of lemonade,
Aerating the tops of trees
And bringing songbirds.
Her wand is the vacuum cleaner,
The polisher, the shoe-shine brush;
She absorbs rubbish,
Gives the sky a wash down.
But her laughter and fun,
Seemingly carefree and scatter-brained,
Are but paper thin;
The confetti she sprays
On damsons, cherries and plums
Quiver in tail-end winter winds,
Which bring to roost
The fine lines between seasons.

3. SUMMER

Summer is lazily languid:
She comes and she lasts,
And lasts as long as she sleeps.
See her dozing on the riverbank,
Stretching in the hedgerows,
Lying amongst the grasses and the flowerbeds.

But seldom does she stay:
Storms blow her away,
Rip leaves off trees,
Pelt dust into heavy glue,
Make the leaking summer house a refuge
For parasols and stacked-up plastic chairs.
Then she creeps back
Oblivious to the damage,
Innocently sleeps again,
And impinges upon autumn.

4. AUTUMN

Autumn is many-fold:
She is the reason for this year's harvest,
The seed for next;
She is the end, the beginning.
She has on one side
The ovens of summer,
And on the other
The storing, the cleaning up,
The hygiene of winter.
She is more besides:
She ripens to maturity
The rough finishes of summer;
She is the farewell to migrating birds,
The comfort to falling leaves.
She is the wise one,
The hub of all seasons.

THE SWAN

In spring
mother swan,
With father looking on,
Shows off her babies
In tow behind her
One by one.

In summer
Cool
In the pool.

October
In flight,
A magnificent sight.

Winter
Each flake of snow
Reminds me of her so.

Tell me, swan,
How can I, like you,
Please everyone.

LET THE WIND BLOW

Let the wind blow
For you and me,
Let the wind blow
For the farmer to see
His wet corn blow
Healthily;
Let the wind blow.

Let the wind blow
For you and me,
Let the wind blow
For the lofty tree
To feel the leaves blow
Fitfully;
Let the wind blow.

Let the wind blow
For you and me,
Let the wind blow
To set the perfume free,
As the flower heads blow
Heartily;
Let the wind blow.

Let the wind blow
For you and me,
Let the wind blow
For the children to see
The pond yachts blow
Majestically;
Let the wind blow.

Let the wind blow
For you and me,
Let the wind blow
For the farmer's corn,
Let the wind blow
For the leaves on the tree,
Let the wind blow.

Let the wind blow
For the wild sunny flowers,
Let the wind blow
For the yachts on the pond,
Let the wind blow,
Especially,
For you and me.

LIFE

Life can be defined in a hundred different ways
By a hundred different people;
But let us narrow it down.
Let us say it is the period between
When we are born
And when we are physically dead.
We can all recognize this
Without complications of beliefs and disbeliefs,
The beforehands and the hereafters,
And has the advantage of positive witness
By those about us.

What do we find?
Like a magnet comprises a piece of iron
And that invisible, magical something else,
So life has two elements:
A body, a moving existence,
That can see and be seen,
Can touch and be touched;
And also that invisible something else,
A mind, a soul, a thinking process
That seems to operate from within
And extends to everywhere outside.

Both bind together into a single entity,
A human, a person uniquely shaped in thought and substance,
And in so being
Senses the extremities of the environment,
Reaches out, experiments, moves on,
Instantly recognizes other people
And the hierarchical concerns that permeate society;
And in truth
Has a hard core of selfishness, envy and greed
To support it,
Which is hidden to all outside itself.

But what of benevolence and charity,
The utopian cups of plenty filled to overflowing?
What of the capacity to co-operate and not compete,
To combine strength with strength
And skill with skill,
To add and not to take away?
Perhaps in some extended life
These will be satisfied,
And there will be blossoms and scent
And cloudless skies
And intoxicating goodwill to all men.

THE FEBRUARY TREE

In the wood
The tree in February
Is tall,
And crowned with filigreed
Intricate lace.

It has a shape,
A height, a girth
All its own;
It breaths
And has a heart and soul.

If it were to speak,
This time would be appropriate
For it to say,
"I am me,
I have my own identity."

And it would sadly sigh
As its burgeoning buds
And clusters of entanglement
Begin to merge with all the rest
Into a season of anonymity.

THESE PEOPLE

Who are these people
Who philosophise over rhubarb leaves,
Who pick a situation from the ground,
Decorate it with air and verbiage
And float it as a *magnum opus*?

Who are these people
Who can measure a piece of string,
Tie it into complicated knots,
Unravel it with dexterity
And find its length unchanged?

The world is full of them;
Great ambitions, tiny shallow minds,
Who play about with mighty words,
Deep, sonorous, long, calculated words,
And rarely scratch the surface.

Do they have homes to go to,
Wives, houses, cats and kids?
How interesting surely it would be
To take the lid off their domestic life
And watch them pee!

BANK HOLIDAY

I can't be bothered
To cross the bridge
To mix with other folk.

Let today instead
Be a day that never was,
That stands still because
There is no compulsion
To do other
Than stay here in the sun,
Speak to no one,
Bathe in warmth,
And let hours trickle away
Imperceptibly.

Things from yesterday
Wait to be done,
And other things will come,
Exciting things, boring things.

Let them wait
Whilst I luxuriate,
Wrap myself in the glory
That is everything and nothing,
Watch dandelion seeds
Fluff across the path
And spawn in lawns
Without trying to sweep them up.

Let price tags, crisp bags
Flap about in draughts of passing cars,
Swirl amongst the cherry blossoms
Littering the tarmac drive.

Let them pile in corners
For a good while yet
Till the sun sets,
And the Bank Holiday begets
Tomorrow.

PLANNING AUTHORITY

Did Hadrian at all
Get consent to install
His wall,
Or, Offa his dyke?

I did, I recall,
When building a stall
For my bike.

SUNDAY

It is a winding-down
Or a preparing-to-start day,
A finishing-off or a commencing day,
The end or the beginning;
It is not the middle,
It is a yesterday or a tomorrow day,
It is not a today day.

Its heart is in last week
Or next,
A part of the past or the future,
Not the present;
It is not a stand-by-itself day.

It is an in-between,
A non-existent day,
A long-lasting waste of time
Which over a lifespan
Consumes ten years,
Seeming like twenty
But actually no time at all.

HARVEST FESTIVAL

The space where the congregation sits
Is full;
Between that and the vaulted roof
Hangs the heavy scent of autumn.
A drunken wasp trying to get out
Climbs the stained-glass window.

A melon from Sainsbury's
Sits alongside apples and pears
And sticks of rhubarb;
A bit of posh wrapping paper divides them.

He who came with nothing
Will take something away;
She who is sick at home
Will get a belated visit,
And a half-pound of grapes and a peach
With the price tags taken off.

Everyone is happy;
But remember next year
The melon should be cut in four,
To avoid the squabbling.

TWO BLACKBIRDS

I saw two blackbirds here today
Feeding their young;
It must be spring and welcoming,
Though I need to say
Five years it is since they were here,
Five bleak years:
No song, no singing, no pleasure bringing,
No fledglings reared.

I wonder why;
Many experts give reasons,
Reasons I can understand:
Absence of margins
When the fields are ploughed,
Torn up hedges, fertilizer, insecticide,
The ozone layer, deforestation,
All caused by man's intrusion.

But are these notions too simplistic,
Better studied in the round;
Isn't the whole of life's experience
More profound,
And these intrusions
Forming but a part,
Slowly unfurling,
The evolution of the natural world?

Such evolution saw
Branches come to trees,
And birds grow wings to fly,
And fishes learned to shelter in the reeds
When the sun was high.
I saw fine-fettled blackbirds here today
Feeding their young, suffice to say
That spring is here and welcoming.

POVERTY STRICKEN

Five pounds for a packet of fags,
No wonder our children are dressed in rags!

Five of us here smoke a packet a day,
That's twenty-five pounds we have to pay.

No wonder our children are dressed in rags,
When it costs five pounds for a packet of fags.

THE GARDEN PARTY

Is it true
Mr Trilby
Will be there?

Is it true Mr Trilby
With all his attributes will be,
Is it true
Mr Trilby
Will be there?

Is it true
That crowds of people stare
For they've heard
That Mr Trilby
Will be there?
And tickets have been sold
Whether the day be hot or cold,
Because everyone's been told
That the redoubtable Mr Trilby
Will be,
The redoubtable Mr Trilby
Will be there.

Why *Mr Trilby*
You may say.
He hasn't worn a hat
For many a day.
He is called Mr Trilby
Because it rhymes with 'will be',
And no other word
Would fit it anyway.

PURE JOY

It doesn't start as a noise starts
With a sudden rude interruption;
It doesn't come as a storm comes
With a bolt of rain from the blue;
It doesn't grow as a master plan
From successive thought.

It does not intrude;
It is here for the deserving.
It is not restrictive
To place or being or circumstance.
Its presence is momentary,
But its echoes last forever.

MAN IN A RUT

In this great wide land
He has dug with his hands
A deep narrow pit,
And piled on either side
The spoil to build two mountains,
Between which he lives.
The world and heavy trucks
Go by and round him:
He ignores them.

His life is with the worms
And with familiar things.
He squirms
At even the smallest hint
Of something new,
Of something his parents,
If they were here,
Wouldn't know, wouldn't recognize,
Wouldn't understand.

But change is inherent:
Machinery comes, earth moving, thought shifting,
And from the flattened site
New structures grow
That cast light
And insight
Into far horizons,
That bedazzle and attract
Those hungry people reaching for the sky.

He digs deeper through the rubble
Where he feels the intimate touch
Of homely earth.
Why others burst about him
And self destruct, he doesn't ask.

He is a man with his own mission,
He is a happy man;
Others may say he is nondescript,
And he wouldn't disagree.

THE SKYLARK

I last saw a scyther scythe
At the side of the road
At Llanfairfechan.
The scyther saw a skylark there
And left the long grass lest
It should disturb the skylark's nest.

The foreman came to the pub to ask
Why he'd not finished his lowly task.
The scyther pointed to the sky:
No other words were needed to answer why.

MODERN TIMES

There is no romance
In candles and wine,
When the storm outside
Cuts the power line,
And everywhere is cold
And dark and miserable;
When potatoes stop boiling
And bacon fat congeals,
When the cheese sandwich
Cobbled together for a meal
Sticks in the throat,
And one walks about
In an overcoat.

What use now
Without the oil,
The oil lamp polished to perfection,
The copper kettle
Perched above the settle,
The antique spit
Decorated with artificial flowers
And set in rustic brick?

What use that Neil Armstrong
Should walk upon the moon,
Doing his giant leap for mankind,
When the man outside
Has only to climb eighteen feet
In the wind and sleet,
But is still unable
To fix the cable?!

THE GIFT

If you refuse it
It becomes forever out of reach,
Growing with an attraction
And an importance
That hadn't been there before.

It mocks you,
Scorns and teases you
Till you feel inadequate,
And your guilt
Bursts out and breaks away.

If you accept it,
Even though it be hideous,
You can at least pretend
A show of gratitude
And gradually move it out of sight.

VIOLIN CONCERTO

I am the voice,
The voice and conscience;
I am the violin
That stands above the rest;
I suffer no compromise,
I build up strength to shout,
To shout loud in protest;
I am not, I don't want to be,
A part of this gathering.

I hover above the fusion
Of percussions,
Cello, double bass,
And like a meadow lark
Take wings; I fly
Into the upper reaches of the sky.

I dance and flirt;
I feather the conductor's baton
With the air of independence,
Till it pulls me back
Down into the maelstrom,
Compressing me into a shape
That isn't me at all.

This surely can't be me
Solo-being that I am;
Happiest skimming
The fresh untrammelled hills
In the early morning,
Breathing in
Time and great distance,
Where I can weave new tracks
And trace aeroplane vapours into space.

Damn the conspiracy!
The cacophony
Turns blacks and whites
Into mongrel shades of grey;
Even tubular bells
Are fettered with the entrails
Of the tenor horn.

And again I am pitched
Into stormy seas,
Just to please an audience
Shuffling in their seats,
Assuming intellects and imaginations
Which they have not got.
Waiting for the bar to open
At the interval.

Away, away I go again,
Light and tingly,
Seeking my own intoxication
In the stars;
This time
I shall not come back.

THE CARAVAN

The desert is no ordinary desert:
All sand has blown away,
Its surface hard and crisp,
A dirty white,
Like the inside skin
Of dried-out oranges.

In the rainy season
He comes out of his caravan,
Arranges on the ground an empty peach tin,
An iron long-handled pan,
A bowler hat propped up between two bricks
And lined with tin foil to make it leakproof.

He strips off his clothes,
Dances a naked dance,
Lifts his head up to the sky
And lets the rain gurgle in his throat:
At that moment he is nearer to heaven
Than he is to earth.

Next day to keep the dust out
And the evaporation in,
He collects the pots,
Stores them under the van,
And covers them with corrugated iron sheets
Previously dumped in the wasteland.

Other nourishment he gets from helicopter drops;
Cucumber juice flows from airborne pipes,
And that which overflows
Dries into sticky lumps,
And he licks them off as he would a lollipop,
To satisfy his immediate need.

Back in the caravan
He draws the curtain on the only window,
Sits at the table next to his brother
And thanks God that the harvest is in,
His brother does not respond:
He has been dead all of five months.

REMEMBRANCE

You ask that I remember you;
I will.
You ask that I remember you,
For all the reasons you want to be
Remembered for,
And I will –
If you will tell me
What they are.

ON READING *ANTIQUES TRADE GAZETTE*

It is like having a bath;
It unfolds a timeless world beneath the grime
Where cameos come alive
And interweave one with the other
Making a nonsense of chronology,
Where fact and fancy blend,
Where cold reality warms
To the romance of history and imagination.

Pink perfume rather than time
Is of the essence;
Limbs glow
With the soft caress of Knight's Castile,
And towel-wrapped Leonardo DiCaprio
Reflects mistily in the mirror,
Obliterating the sciatica,
The abject poverty of thought and everyday living,
Where morning spreads into the afternoon
And even into the evening.

The printed pages turn;
Victorian velours hang at the windows
Overlooking the tennis lawn,
Belatedly shading the sun
From the dusky velvet-seated dining chairs
And Georgian gate-legged table.
Children in knickerbockers,
Gilt framed,
Apple faced and innocent,
Lean against the sober Italian credenza.

Dutch marquetry sits between Jacobean oak
And Edwardian satinwood secretaire;
Venetian glass vies with Worcester porcelain,
And on the walls
Drape Persian carpets and musty Indian rugs
Spiced with incense from the Orient.
The French ormolu clock on the mantlepiece
Chimes the centuries away.

It is suddenly the last page;
Advertisers' announcements – no pictures,
And a draught
Comes in from outside.

SECRET LOVE

I feel it
In every limb,
In every thought
As fate begins
To shuffle lives about again.

I see it
In trees, in hills
As weeks go by
And arbours fill
With daffodils.

I hear it
Loud across the street
And at the crossroads
Where pathways meet
And conscience wants to face defeat.

I sense it
All about the ballroom floor,
And wise men
Taking tickets at the door
No doubt have seen it all before.

REQUIEM

Someone came to me when I was ill
And dying
And gave me a pill.
It wasn't God
But a nurse who was passing by
With her trolley.
I remember she said,
"He hasn't got long. Get the porter,
We need the bed."

They sent me in a bag
To Liverpool Lime Street
For students to cut me up;
I gave no one a chance
To think of me in church,
I didn't believe in it.

Perhaps now I am in heaven,
Perhaps not.
Whatever,
I lived, I loved,
I had enjoyment;
I had sorrow.
I will remember you all –
Tomorrow.

THE ALLIGATOR

A Catholic priest
Was the first feast,
But it was the seasoned Spanish waiter
Who gave the alligator
Indigestion,
Provoking the question:
Would an Italian
Make it well again?

But maybe an English peasant
Would be more tender than a pheasant,
Or even a Greek tourist
Would cure it.
But instead of all these
And because we are in the Antipodes,
An Australian geezer
Would be easier.

It is so difficult to cater
For an alligator!

RESURRECTION

You destroyed me,
And for that I thank you.
You walked in, took everything I had,
Stripped me naked and went.

I was a soul in shock,
Arms, feet, feelings numb,
A cabbage for a mind,
Left to rot on the midden.

I thank you;
There is so much more
Now that you have gone.
I am alive again,
And reawakened
To a world I had forgotten.
It is for this
That I thank you.

THE PLOTTERS

On a silvery night
When the moon is bright,
When the November trees
Have lost their leaves,
In a quiet spot,
In the quiet space,
They hatch a plot
For peace to embrace
The whole of the universe.

WHAT IS TRUTH?

Is it truth, or what is it
When evidence of the happening
Sits close to hand,
Fits like a comfortable glove,
But seems too convenient by far?

Although I know sight sees
And hearing hears,
They both hold
To the mind's-eye view
And self-deception.

You say you see the sunshine,
And at night
When the moon and stars are out,
You see the way clearly;
I see only thunderstorms.

You feel in the morning
The euphoria, the happiness;
I sense the lurking,
The murkiness
Of rank despair.

THE FOX

All day
And deep into the night
The hurt dominates.

The hoar frost
And the full moon
Concentrate on the open wound,
Like pins
Pricking into raw flesh.

Nothing now
But thin wind;
No desire to play,
To lay fake scent
In and out the brook;
Only the wish
For a long last stretch
In that final private place,
Where bluebells will come in spring
With lesser celandine,
Where wild anemone
Will spread its intricacy
Across the woodland floor.

The frost freezes hard,
The wind dies,
The moon glides slowly
Behind wisps of cloud;
There is silence.

TABLETS OF STONE

Truth is transient:
It clings to a situation
Only until the circumstances change,
Until conventions become too difficult,
Until the wine's bouquet turns sour.

It then moves on
To its new persuasion;
Rewrites itself,
Is worshipped and sung about
In all new places.

It leaves behind
A set of wisdoms,
A bible of ambiguities,
Bland words of sunshine and disaster
In one event.

As time passes, wheat and chaff
Become indistinguishable one from the other,
And birds pick out the pieces
That suit them best,
And wait for the next delivery.

EQUALITY (1)

Released from freedom,
Bound instead with compromise,
No rich, no poor,
Saints or sinners.

A time of conglomerations
And innovations
Turning idiots and Socrates
Into mediocrity,
Making a safe, predictable, equal,
Unexciting world
Of cabbages and potatoes.

THE TABLE LAMP

Much like a woman,
No matter how uncanny,
It gets itself turned on
In company.
Even more like a woman
At bedtime, without a hitch,
It gets turned off
At the flick of a switch.

IN MEMORIAM

In the graveyard
Dead flowers in wire bins
Are the only things
That are seen to decay.

The rest
Like coatings of paint
Keep fresh the images of folk
Who want to slip away.

Cold slabs,
Giant yews
Planted to hold in memories
Cling like yesterday.

All enclosed
In black crimped iron railings,
Guarding them from
The intrusions of today.

A dead flower
In a rusty iron bin
Is the only memorial
That is appropriate.

PAIN

There is something simply shouting in my mind
As I wait at the corner;
It swells and makes me almost blind
And sweat as if I'm in a sauna.
When yellow ducks fly past from Interpol
I know I'm into more than Panadol!

LOVE

It lies in long grass,
In dead leaves,
Where the hedge roots
Tie their knots
In the sandy bank.

It lies where it is seen
By warm winds ruffling its hair,
And trespassers, creeping by
With envious glance
And shamed intrusion.

It thrills at its own completeness,
Enwrapped limbs and murmuring hearts
Seeking and being nothing but themselves,
With the rest of the world
Passing by, like ships at sea.

AMBULANCE

I am seventy-two,
It doesn't look
As if I'll ever be
Seventy-three!

THE COLLECTOR

After the affray,
Having stood all day,
Proudly he sat in his chair
Bought from the antiques fair;
Whilst woodworm as they must
Turned his finery into dust.

NIGHT AND DAY

Do you choose night instead of day
When moon at its height
Gives light
That is black and white?
Other colours,
Even grey, would be an intrusion
Into the pencil sketch
Of square church tower
With poplar trees behind,
And haunting hints
Creeping round each shape,
Each secret sound.

Or choose the day,
The scintillating summer's day,
When sunflowers sway
In warm winds,
And play
'Catch me if you can'
With angry bees,
Where midday trees
Can't hold the shade
Of tangled leaves,
Across the pond
Where marigolds belong,
And lazy carp do linger long?

To choose between
Would be to denigrate,
To throw askew
The balance of the two;
To ask for sleep
Never to be awakened,
Wakefulness
Never to be offered rest:
The two are tied
Inseparably.

THE WAIT

Ships across the bay
Sway at anchor,
Angry clouds assemble,
Tree tops tremble;
The storm is imminent.

Patrons wait
In orchestra stalls
For the curtain call;
Nerve ends twitch,
Coughs are stifled.

The sky at dawn
Yawns for the darkness to shift,
Pregnant moments
Before the sun lifts
Into day.

Each scene completes itself:
In comes the wind and rain,
The overture,
The morning looking much the same
As yesterday.

Why so predictable?
Why not some new aspiration
An eloquence, a fragrance
To drown out
The monotony?

THE BLACKBIRD

Like a lorry on a hill
My mind stands still,
Overheated.

Noisy gears cease to labour,
Brakes savour
A moment's eminence
To allow the environs to intrude –
An interlude
For reflection,
For picking up the speck of dust
And giving it wings
And things
To get it over the hill,
Experience the thrill,
The trill,
Of a blackbird singing.

BEGINNINGS AND ENDS

I remember hearing
Beaches counting pebbles
As the tide came in,
And the drags
As it went out again.

I remember
Seagulls' wings being battered
At the height of the storm,
And the quietness
That came after.

I remember
Guillemots' eggs being hatched
In the cliffs above Holyhead,
And old birds
Floating dead in the sea.

I remember seagrass,
Its first green tufts being trampled
In the spring,
And its dreary, withered, long untidiness
In winter.

I remember
The first fresh paint
On beach huts,
And the wet mould and wood lice
As it peeled off.

I remember emotions,
Clean, open, far-flung,
At the beginning of the season;
Withdrawn, shifty, humpbacked
When it was time to go.

I remember
The beginnings and the ends,
The substantial in-betweens
Completely obliterated,
Left only to the imagination.

WITH AN APOLOGY TO MAURICE POE

The school register says:
Poe, M.
What a gem!
Is it any wonder
They call him
The rhyming 'guzunder'?

THE MENU

(From the Dictionary of Indigestion)

The waiter turned to me and said:
A medley of well-chopped mushrooms
In a peppercorn parsley sauce
With a frolic of iced fresh radish
And pickled chive, of course.

To follow –
A pork Pavarotti,
A symphony of sausage melange,
A meander of nuts and pink mayonnaise
And a thrill of lemon pottage.
For dessert –

A moment of mint meringue
In a boat of chocolate eclair
With waves of cold cream custard
Round an island of Worcestershire pear.

To conclude –
A finale of Kenyan coffee
With a floating of double cream
And almond and brandy liqueurs
And a taste of the in-between.

QUALITY TIME

Silence, like still water,
Is fragile and easily broken
By even the smallest distraction,
A crack of light in a darkened room,
A tingling of the skin.

For silence is not just the absence of noise,
But the shut-off of physicality
To allow the mind a freedom without bias,
To explore its own environment,
However short the time.

THE WIDOWER

Two is company
Three is a crowd,
Where does that put the widower?
Alone
In company
In a crowd?

THE LAST DAY

They stood on the ridge
Rising up from the flat land,
And looked out to sea.

A high wind was blowing,
Rain was forecast,
There was nowhere to shelter.

Then the rains came,
Thrown as if by the sea
In a fit of madness.

But they were at a standstill,
Their own quarrel had drained from them
All emotion.

They did not see,
Nor did they wish to see,
The hint of sunlight.

ANOTHER DAY

Windows without walls
And walls
Where windows once had been;
A new shape,
Another reason why;
A new perspective,
Another door shut upon the past,
And another opening upon the future.

THE POET

If actions speak louder than words
Then the poet at best
Is a whisperer,
And at worst
A silent mute.

THE DOG

But for the barking dog at my heels,
I'd hitch my gear and take a ride
On the sun now sinking below Abbeyford Bridge.

With that in mind I take my dog
And leash him to his favourite store,
Where he will find food and drink galore.

Back at the bridge the sun is gone,
It is dark and I am alone,
Except for the whimperings in my soul.

He lifts his tail, he licks my hand,
Then leads the way down the shabby street,
As we return to the empty flat.

THE TREE

After the storm
The tree is a clown,
A drunkard fallen down,
His long, straight hair
Scattered everywhere,
His limbs *akimbo.*

Why should it be
When alive a tree,
But when it's dead
A man instead?

IT

I wish it would go away,
In fact, disappear forever.
If time could go back,
That it be cut off at source,
That it had never existed,
Not even a passing thought.

Should I put it in a box,
Place it on the highest shelf,
Let it gather dust, decay,
Fall apart, disintegrate?
Oh, how I have tried
Again and again, how I have tried!

It would not be ignored
Or go away of its own volition
Or be destroyed. Instead it grows
Like fungus on a dead tree root.
And then I know what I have always known,
It was and is a part of me.

THE LAST STORY

There is a story in every blade of grass,
In every feather of every bird,
In every letter of every word.

There is a story in every weave of cloth,
In every flicker of every light,
In every bit of black and white.

There is a story in every finger tip;
In each perception of every mind
There is a find.

Nature being what it is
These stories will be seen only when we
are blind,
Heard only when we are deaf,
Felt when emotions are worn away through
age and pain.

BEDLAM

Is that a song I heard,
The song of a bird?
Surely not, for I am alone,
Alone in this shell of a room,
With four grey walls
And windows barred.

When I say I am alone,
I mean with myself;
But there are other people here,
Three kinds of people,
All very different,
And many rooms.

The song of the bird
Would certainly not be heard
By the establishment,
The medical orderlies, who patrol
Like prison guards in white coats,
Exuding carbolic soap and chloroform.

The second group
Would hear it as a rallying cry;
Social workers being centred within themselves
Will use anything as an excuse
To extol their own philosophy.

The third group are the residents,
We call ourselves individuals;
Therefore I speak for myself when I ask,
Was it a song I heard,
A song of a bird?
For my wife Kitty was a bird!

A WINTER'S TALE

When the leaves have dropped and the larder is full
And the door is shut against the cold,
The world comes down to a single room,
To a solitary confine.

The days are lonely, lastingly long
Despite the shortened daylight hours,
And the mind being tied to the little room
Is fretfully impatient.

Out there the thin grey sky is stretched
To limits of transparency,
And flat enough to sketch upon
With painted pencilled wings.

Frozen monotony
And unfettered truths
Drench dark corners, crannies and cracks
In street-lamped afternoons.

So be it when the door re-opens
And thoughts return from the bleak outside,
The room's festooned with winter cheer
And with no burst pipes.

THE ARCHWAY

Silent and dark it beckons me through,
Though it be fraught with poisoned daggers and darts,
And dungeons haunt the dank, deep water holes
Where fish won't come.

And there the trees curl up their leaves
Against the vicious wind,
The sky is blue, the blue of tinted ice
In foreign lands.

But still the archway calls and I am drawn
Through the screen of honeysuckle dew
And thrown amongst the clutch of bramble thorn,
While the Scylla face of the wild dog rose
Sheds crops of crocodile tears.

OPERA

At home we woo and are wooed in the nude
But when we go out we flaunt
Armani suits, and act and look,
And indeed, we are the height of elegance.

Haute coutured, manicured,
Tied and tailed, taxis hailed;
Lulled in the intervals and at the end
Into canapés and aperitifs.

And salmon mousse forked up loose,
With a haze of mayonnaise,
And sirloin steaks lightly raked
Over charcoal grills.

Then –
Coffee Italienne!
And when we get home, let's face it,
Again we are naked.

THE BIG FISH

The highest position glistens,
Its own halo
A concentration, a spectrum
Above the rest.

There is room for only one,
A precarious existence,
Thin and narrow,
Trembling with jostlings from below.

And when he falls
There is nowhere for him to cling
Or bring any semblance of dignity
To his situation.

The fish in the pond
Who were his worshippers
Are slippery and elusive,
Pretending not to see or comprehend.

TULIP GRASS

It was June:
The tulip grass had grown tall;
At night,
It stuck out from the side of the moon.

Music came from quadraphones.
Soundless music, emitting thought
That shot like fountains of fireworks
Bursting multi-coloured and quickly dying.

Wisps of cloud disguised as a horse's mane
Diffused the light on earth,
To awake the child
From its nest of green bracken.

The child kicked at the womb
From which it had been prematurely ejected
To find it wasn't there.

Instead it found the voice the music had lost
In its flirtation with celestial things,
And it yelled.

THE COLOUR GREY

Why is grey dull?
It seems to apply so much to old age,
Grey hair, grey personality,
Grey pullover on narrow shoulders
Leaning towards the fire
On winter nights.

Is grey old age
And old age dull,
To be put in a drawer and forgotten
Alongside flannelette sheets and shirts
And vests and long johns,
Until come across by the next generation
Frantically searching for the will?

HARMONY

Point, counterpoint,
Needles pointing into opposite directions,
Pricking the meanings of principle apart;
The fundamental issues.

Machinery turns, blends and bleeds,
Its blood trickling downwards to the centre,
To join and set
Into waxes of wisdom.

THE STRANGER

He came unexpected,
Like a wisp of cloud,
Like a silence from a loud noise,
Untrumpeted from an inconspicuous place,
A giant from a nebula of gnats.

He came dry out of the sea,
Hot from the refrigerator,
Lifting up from the altar
Bold and Bibleless,
Unholy and with authority.

He put into words
Sounds and rhythms from unheard murmurings,
He mustered thoughts which had roamed untamed
In the periphery.

Now he is gone,
The challenge is to understand.

CIVILIZATION

The elephant came into the garden
And sang the *Hallelujah Chorus*,
And before it went it left a tiger trap,
But no tiger came,
Because we are civilized.

We search instead for bombs in passages,
Or unattended luggage at railway stations,
Or spiked shoes at airports,
Or primed dilapidated cars in one-way streets,
Or a pregnant woman in a busy restaurant
With explosives and nails in her corset
Instead of a baby,
For we are civilized!

POPPIES

Think,
Think field,
Field full of poppies,
Poppies growing,
Growing, blowing both ways, in the wind.

Think,
Think Flanders,
Flanders, heroism;
Think Afghanistan, crops harvested
Destined for the streets of London.

Think,
Think death,
Death in Belgium's fields,
Death manufactured,
Manufactured in laboratories.

Think,
Think poppies,
Poppies growing, blowing,
Blowing both ways in the fields,
The fields of glory and of ignominy.

SAINTLY SINNER

He sneezed a big sneeze
And he was dead:
It was said
He had choked on his own vomit.

Thus, he had died,
Just as he had lived,
Straightforward, no fuss, no complications.
A model of simplicity.

Although in death one grows cold,
Grows stiff and has a vacant stare,
He seemed relaxed,
At peace with himself.

Nevertheless, it was the end –
But not quite:
Seven women wonder
As they gather round.

BALLET

(A poem in three parts)

1. MANY MANSIONS

Of swept clean paths,
Lawns neat-edged,
Borders carefully tended,
A microcosm of conformity:
Birth and death
And all that comes between,
Like going to church on Sunday.

Of naked feet
Dancing in field of wet grass,
Of coiffured hair let loose
And like a caged bird set free
Tossing celebratorily in the wind.

Of shelter under the umbrella tree,
That collects the rain on its flat, fat
fingers,
Then drips invisibly
Onto the forest floor,
And in deep, dark blotches
On the cuffs and shoulders
Of the cream silk blouse,
Whilst going to church on Sunday.

Of mountains climbed
And mountain peaks
That tremble to the touch of new
experience,
Of limbs converging into wooded slopes,
To valley of intrigue
And everlasting enchantment.

2. THE DANDELION STEM

I have searched,
I have found;
Let me in,
For it is cold outside:
Grass is stiff,
The birds are frozen on the wing:
My innocence has gone.

If proof you need
I will break in,
Display the animal instinct
You accuse me of not having.

You do not respond:
You think I will go away.
I break in,
Desperate like a hungry man:
We feast.

We feel the orgasmic tide
Straightway ripple across the sand,
Gather strength on the rocks,
Crash white hot on the cliff face,
A torturous contradiction of the Antichrist
That brings out the passion at bloom
From the bitter stem of the dandelion.

3. DEEP PURPLE

The straight line widens into a path,
Into a track,
Into a broad expanse of roadway;
Hints of colour to pastel shades,
To striking richness;
Short pricks of sound, increasing in
length
To incessant noise.

Knowledge is such,
A progression through thought,
Through experience,
Through labouring hands along the way.

But wisdom is one step beyond:
It is the juice of the fruit,
The distillation,
Not easily absorbed in a society
Preoccupying itself with compromise
In its search for equality
Amongst diverse aspirations.

Wisdom is the one step beyond,
Whereon lies the carpet of deep purple,
The deep purple of truth
And of going to church on Sunday.

THE CHAIR MENDER

He was small,
He wore glasses,
He was trodden on.
He had a workshop,
An eye for beauty,
Strong forearms,
Delicate fingers
That could feel and sense and search out
The wonderful shapes of things.

When he brought it in
Its legs were scratched,
Arms loose, knocked about;
But it was a thing of beauty.

He worked through the night,
The next night and the next,
It was awkward to handle;
When he moved it onto the table
It hit him in the eye,
Kicked him on the shin,
As a human would.

He got impatient,
But as he looked at it,
Stripped of its filth,
Its beauty shone,
Its majestic haughtiness
Sent quivers through his fingers
Into his spine.

He concentrated the more;
He smoothed rough patches,
Smeared nutritious oils
Into scratches and knocks,
Feathered his fingers into curves and
crevices.

It was said
The bigger the challenge the greater the
rewards.
Thank God he worked through the night,
Padlocked in the room at the back
Away from prying eyes.

He was missed in the pub
Because of the empty seat;
He had never really spoken to anyone.

They said he had a tumbledown shed
On the trading estate,
He often slept there
But he had never missed his pint.
Was he ill?
Perhaps someone should call.

The ambulance came,
Sirens blared,
They handled the object with concern,
He asked them to be careful
With his masterpiece.
He was the craftsman,
The new generation,
He recycled, sustained and customized,
Let nothing rot,
Threw nothing away.

He turned,
He saw the shattered padlock;
He was small,
He wore glasses,
They didn't understand
He had an eye for beauty,
Delicate fingers
That could feel and sense and search out
The wonderful shapes of things.
The handcuffs were ugly,
Too big for his small wrists.

HOSPICE

The ones who love me I am sending them away
For I know what it's like to love
And watch and wait,
And weep and feel helpless
When needed most.

I wish for none of this,
I choose to be alone
And will know them as they really are.
When the time comes
I will wish for them happiness
With no regrets
For having known me –
Farewell, we shall never meet again.

THE FOOT OF THE TREE

The lion waits:
I climb high.
Dawn breaks,
The lion yawns:
I climb higher still.

Vultures flap,
Slap their wings,
And like the lion,
Wait.

Daylight takes the dark away
To somewhere inaccessible,
The lion swipes,
Vultures hop.

I fall at the lion's feet.
The lion seeing only skin and bone
Contemptuously turns away,
The vultures follow.

Giant ants swarm;
The tree is tall and far away
Like an absent friend.

TWO FACED

Sybil had a hat
That made her face look flat,
She changed it for another and found
Her face was round.
Which suited most
The grinning apple
Or the piece of toast?

NEW DIMENSION

We live,
We die;
When death,
Like life,
Has run its course
What then?

COMMERCIAL TRAVELLER

Lying here
After it has all finished,
And the futility of it all
Sets in;
A naked arm
Reaches up, stretches to nowhere,
Balances,
Falls neither forwards nor backwards
And is weightless.

Whatever it was,
The urgency, the brute instinct,
Might now never have been,
A promise so saturated in itself,
Its coming and going
Leaves only bewilderment:
The overnight bag needs packing,
And the orders phoning through.

Yet inexplicably,
The arm loses its equilibrium
And falls down onto the naked thigh,
And the urgency, the instinct
Is back.

On scented pond
The water lily lies,
And in the warmth
Its flower unfolds again
With a hint of morning dew.

THE END

When it's twenty-four hours to sunset
And only one hour to live,
Does it matter what the sunset promises
Or has to give?

BLINDNESS (2)

I have what I require:
A room that's warm in winter,
With a view of a wood still there
Though I cannot see it.
I have a bookcase with books of familiar feel,
And a settee
With memories maybe
And pictures on the wall of family.

I have a pipe rack on the mantlepiece,
A rocking chair with soft cushion,
And comfortable slippers on the hearth,
And on Radio 3
A piano piece by Schumann
Spans the extremities of imagination,
Oh, how I wish that this were true!

LEAVE US BE

Darkness begins to fall at four o'clock;
Village tentacles, that all day had stretched
In widening circumference, now retreat
From Brackenberry Wood and country lane which splits
The water meadow from the field of wheat,
And to the south where the peat beds touch the moors:
All of them left to the safety of the night,
So leave them be.

The steeple and the two tall trees gaze
Across the thatch and stone of ancient roofs;
Still and quiet, villagers sleep
Beneath familiar, pock-marked attic space,
But mocking laughter invades their shallow dreams,
For social engineering tries to overcome
The evolution of a thousand years,
With prospects of affordable homes.

Leave us be please, leave us be
To grow or die naturally.

THE MESSAGE

Late autumn says something to me;
When the trees are lean and the days are short,
And the wind comes tunnelling from the east,
When the world becomes a smaller place
Confined to one vicinity.

Look and stretch and there will be found
An ocean in the village pond,
And in the little shop, the lure
Of spices from the Orient,
Ordinarily hidden till now.

Late autumn says that one step brings
The whole world to an outstretched hand,
Miniaturisation in its fine detail
Replacing the rawness of the wind
And the greyness of the cold day.

THE LAST MILE

The last mile is the hungry mile
That gnaws at its guts, wanting secretly
To be alone with itself:
Not like anything that happened before.

It has no description
Except its desire to reach the end;
Everything that has gone before
Is enmeshed in this one intent.

The last mile's end
Is not the end of the beginning,
Or the beginning of the end,
It *is* the end.

HAPPINESS (1)

It comes in small doses
Like scent of bluebells
In woodlands in springtime,
Like whirls of seagulls
When tide is upcoming.
A pinprick of starlight.

Happiness is scarce
Like a patch of green
In dry desert sands,
Like water in drought.
Why then is it rendered cheap
And squandered in the marketplace?
Is it axiomatic
To suffer and wallow in gloom?

TRAVELLING BLIND

I see better when my eyes are shut;
The wings of the large bird cut through the air
With grace, with power and with the rhythm of
The boatman rowing from the other side;
The orange of the summer's evening sun,
Sieving through the birch trees to the lawn,
Gathers longer shadows as the night
With imperceptible footsteps closes in.

I can hear more keenly when my eyes are shut;
The blackbird on the pear tree way out back,
Without the intrusion of the gaudy garden shed
Flaunting itself along the wooden fence;
The tractor in the field, the postman's van
Selectively stopping and starting at neighbours' gates,
Building to a climax or otherwise
As it stops outside, or gently fades away.

I can sense more when I shut my eyes,
Smell, taste and touch
That fill the space vacated by my former sight;
There is heavy scent of greenness from the wood
After summer rain; freshness, savouring the lips,
From dew, rising from the sun-rich meadow;
The roughness on the hands of dry-stone walls
Climbing through the heather on familiar hills.

The fulsomeness of travelling the world
Is here within, in technicolour.

THREE FACED

Facing it he forcibly knocked,
And proportionate to the strength of the door,
He loudly knocked and banged again;
The situation, though difficult,
Needed to be faced with confidence,
With courage and morality.

The second, being fierce of eye,
Knocked in similar circumstance;
Then thumped and kicked restlessly,
And cursed and threatened, but fell apart
When the tables were turned, and he was attacked:
Downtrodden he limped away whimpering.

The third sidled quietly to the door,
Looking to left and right and then some more
And more and more before he knocked,
Hoping he would never be heard.
He then slipped away, he had appeared to try;
Perhaps it would now disappear.

Lion and mouse and the in-between,
A paper tiger blustering;
These three belong at different times
To the one being,
Reflecting various behaviours
During the passage of life.

SLOW PROGRESS

Prosperity as its fruits imply
Stands out, exclusive from the rest,
But only if its roots are firm
And stems aspire to reach the sky;
Some look on, jealously cynical,
Others see an example to follow.

However, if the catch-up is attained
It soon is commonplace, taken for granted;
Weeds begin to strangulate,
And insects suck the succour dry;
Then the world awaits to see
Another spirit breaking free.

RINGS

I have one in my forehead
And two in my nose,
I think I'm in bed
And comatose;
But when I awake
God only knows,
I've got four in my ears
And three in my toes.

THE DIVIDE

A plank on end supports the pergola roof,
And brambles smothering the latticed walls
Replaced the scent of jasmine;
But still they came and sat on broken seats,
To quietly muse, or watch their children play
At climbing trees,
Or chasing butterflies, or hiding in
Favourite dens, pretending to make tea
For visiting friends.

A path made by kids in wellington boots
Led from the pergola to the crumbling wall
And weed-strewn river bank,
With flushes of forget-me-nots
And inlets, where the bullrushes grow,
And where swans are nesting;
A boy, adjusting his fishing float,
Sees without noticing the opposite bank,
And casts his worm.

The other bank was straight and neat,
The trees and lawns were manicured
To the nth degree;
The mansion house was on a rise,
Was painted white, immaculate;
But no one came:
From her window looking down
A sad young girl in her dressing gown,
With envy stared.

Before this narrow stretch
The river ran happily;
Now it held its breath,
Conscious of the two extremes,
Laughter and sorrow,
The living and the dead;
Then rushed away to the waterfall
Where all was free again,
Leaving the enigma behind.

THE BIRD

Fred had heard
That to get a bird,
You put peanuts
In a holder
On your shoulder.
Doubting Cyril
Trying it out
Was kissed by a squirrel
On the snout.

BRAINSTORM

The debris from past attempt has cleared away,
The cracks and pitfalls repaired in the widening groove,
That runs like a riverbed to the far horizon:
The landscape refreshed awaits.

Nothing at first, and then it starts to come
In elongated drips, a trickle, a stream,
And then a mighty uncontrol,
As if sturdy lock gates had been breached.

Impossible in the ensuing floodwater
To pan for gold or search for precious gems,
To grasp the shattering splinters of silvery wisps
That flash away to non-existence.

Instead the rush-away, that leaves behind
The malcontent, whose thwarted expectation
Seeks solace in the specks of peripheral light
That illuminate tomorrow's battered dreams.

DIY

What a t'do I had
Fixing the screw
To the ancient bracket
That held the loo.

The cistern I'm certain
Is not straight,
And if you sit on the seat
It'll not carry your weight.

And if breaking your neck
Is not part of your date,
Perhaps a good drenching
Will seal your fate.

Apart from all that
It's a magnificent beast,
For 'twill hold potted plants
At the very least.

SUNDAY'S CHILD

Look down through the window, there to see
Sunday's child dressed impeccably,
Awaiting his parents at the garden gate,
Fervently wishing he was with his mate
Digging for worms on the river bank,
Instead of at church, dark and dank,
That dispels the warmth of morning sun
And puts the fear of God in one.

THE CLOCK

(A Living Will)

If you have a clock
With a hole in its face,
You can start it up
By inserting the key,
And it will go again
Merrily.

I have a hole in my face
And would like to use it to say,
I am old and have had my fill.
If my heart should falter
Do not resuscitate;
Let me die
Naturally.

MIRAGE

Shall I drink the water now?
It is but a whiff away,
A simple scooping hand outstretched
Across the white-hot sand.

Shall I sip the water now
And let it sting pot-cracked lips,
Running off from my swollen tongue
Into the shifting sand?

Shall I drink the water now?
The lake reflects the shimmering sun,
And shallow wavelets wash against
The flatness of the sands.

And now the water is drunk and dried
And rests behind those searching eyes,
While nothing moves but the blistering sun,
The ants, the sand, the flies.

THE QUESTION

If I were you
And you were me,
Would anyone ever
The difference see,
Between you being you
And me being me?

THE IN-BETWEEN

Looking back, I first experienced it
Sitting on what seemed then a tall cliff,
Overlooking the tides in Anglesey.
And again in the dreary room, where on the wide wall
The maps displayed the world to the geography class,
And the sky outside seemed, oh, so attractive.

Time went by, inexorably replaced
By further time; the feeling did not diminish.
But there loomed a metaphorical crossroads,
Whether to pursue my daytime dreams,
Limitless in their extravagant ways,
Or urgently get up and go.

I haven't followed the boats out of Holyhead;
Not used the maps on the wall to travel the world;
Nor have I found contentment sitting about
Letting my thoughts assuage my wanderlust.
Time has caught up and gone, and leaves behind
Not even a scratch on a piece of furniture.

EQUALITY (2)

Equality amongst men is not:
Those who claim it is
Show by this very thought
Inequality.

To have a straight line at birth
Assumptively challenges nature's law,
The negation of family genes
Fused at conception.

To create during life
The equal playing field,
The equal opportunity,
Is an absurdity.

It is impossible to attain;
Like politicians' promises
Made to please the populace
At election time.

But at death, who knows?
Fine dust imperceptibly falls
On familiar furniture,
And uniformly spreads.

RUTH

Her name was Ruth
And to tell the truth
I knew nothing more about her,
But when to speak, she opened her mouth,
I knew she was a Scouser.

SANDCASTLES AND CINDERS

Wind and rain on windows sing
And rattle their drums on window frames,
To keep me awake when no one comes
On lazy, sunless summer days,
Bringing back the memories
Of long gone childhood revelries.

How absorbing to remember things
Like Blackpool Tower and Aquarium,
Stanley Park and boating lake,
Fishing for numbers to win a prize
At the Pleasure Beach, candyfloss,
Roll-a-penny, coconut shies.

Damn and blast! my tea's gone cold,
The crumpets burnt, the telephone call
I should have made at four o'clock,
I've missed, also the news.
The windows rattle even more,
As I scrape the crumpets in the sink.

CONTRARINESS

The day spreads out its unused time
For it to stand by motionless
In never-ending monotony,
Like a desert filled with yellow sand.

Yet days cut corners when time is scarce;
Hours and minutes slip away
Into dark holes seemingly gone,
Unrecoverable despite the work not done.

For time to spread evenly,
It should slow down in busy times,
And speed up when things are slack;
But will this ever be?

LAMENT

Now that I am blind
I hear more,
And sense your body language,
So leave me at home
To be alone,
To wallow in my dotage.

LIGHTNING

Thunder is loud but far away,
And in the middle of the night
Lightning fills the room with brightness,
Then it is darker than before.

How long will it take to harness such power,
To meet the ever increasing needs
Of this, our civilization,
Hungry that we are for progress?

But where in the queue will it have to wait,
For still we cannot direct the rain
To areas of persistent drought,
Or sunshine to a field of corn?

Meantime, impatiently,
It sets the roof of the barn on fire,
Scares the horses out of their wits,
And fatally strikes the apple tree.

THE SUNFLOWER

Quiverings, expectancy
In the warm and sultry atmosphere,
Like a placid lake responding
To advances of the storm.

Shiverings, uncertainty
Behind the facade of indifference
To this pressing situation,
Which will inevitably come to pass.

Fumbling at the first encounter
Like eager puppies newly born,
Fusion of bodies, of personal parts,
Strips away the modesty.

Cryings, deep from the depths within:
Stop, Don't, Don't Stop!
Explosions of rainbow-coloured lights,
A sense of being near to humans.

Fulfilment, calm, competence,
The embryo of a coming life
Proud, secure; intrusion gone,
Flown away to another place.

A ROOM WITH A VIEW

Take me up the stairway to your room,
Please take me up the stairway to your room,
Though the view from there is bare,
At this moment I cannot care,
Please take me up the stairway to your room,
To your room,
Please take me up the stairway to your room.

I haven't got a stairway to my room,
I haven't got a stairway to my room,
Though the view from there is bare
And I couldn't give a care,
I haven't got a stairway to my room,
To my room,
I haven't got a stairway to my room.

Then find another access to your room,
Please find another access to your room,
Where the view from there is bare
And I couldn't give a care,
Please find another access to your room,
To your room,
Please find another access to your room.

I'll find another access to my room,
I'll find another access to my room,
The view from there'll be bare
And I couldn't give a care,
I'll find another access to my room,
I will,
I'll find another access to my room.

HOMECOMING

No one in the morning,
No one there at night,
But sometimes in the afternoon
One gets a fleeting sight,
Of her waving to the ocean
Like a giant bird in flight,
And although there's no one there to greet,
She hopes one day there might.

THE CLOTHES LINE

It sways in the wind as it always swayed
But it has seen the generations change,
From nappies and knickers, to briefs and thongs,
To grown-up bras and stockings and tights;
Then they flew to far-off foreign lands,
Like fledgling chicks from the blackbird's nest.

The concrete clothes post, which always leaned
Towards the house, is disguised now
By a surrounding bush; the lawn and brook
Are much the same, but the banks are terraced;
Most of the old geraniums are gone,
Replaced by home-grown busy Lizzies.

The number of years the sky looked down
Is indeterminable;
But still the wind rushes off the field
To dry the wash, now comprising
Pairs of socks, blue cardigan,
And a shirt with frayed collar and cuffs.

STAIRS

Stairs go up
Or stairs go down
Depending where you stand,
They also tend
To buck the trend
When they go round and round,
I've also seen them waltz, it's true,
When I've had a pint or two.

THE MANSION

Walk, and round the corner you will find,
Behind tall railings and a blackthorn hedge,
A mansion of a most peculiar kind,
Cold, sheer, austere, yet beckoning.

And in the mansion there will be many rooms,
All gloom and mould and dampness, save but one,
Where a vase in the window exudes a light perfume
Of lived-in, warm familiarity.

And through the window on the left you will see
A history of your life condensed,
And on the right a myriad of ways there will be,
From which to choose your destination.

Back on the road I see you hesitate,
The weight of the past astride the future unknown;
But it is not for me to usurp and discount
The blind belief of those who pass me by.

BONFIRE

Midwinter apple prunings;
Reminders in the curls of flame
Of blossoms in the lane,
And lazy drunken wasps
That clung to the last
In apple cores.

But pause,
The damp, the mist, the acrid smoke combine
To form conspiring lines;
A curtain dropping on the past,
Saying at last
That this is another time,
Another day,
That there is no return
To yesterday.

SLOW LANE

How can I feel sorry
For the man in a lorry
When he's jammed in front of me,
Especially when behind I see his brother
In another?

And on my right
A mile-long string
Of these damn things
That get a thrill
By standing still!

SOUTH CHINA SEA

"Water;
Give me water;
Give me water to drink,"
Croaked the parrot:
But there was no water,
And no one left to give it.

Dawn;
Quickly daylight.
The tattered canvas sail
That had been shaped to catch any rain
Was dry:
Another day had begun.

Sea;
Flat, blue
With green streaks,
And white where its cuffs
Lap lazily against the boat:
The sky was brittle with heat.

"Water;
Give me water;
Give me water to drink."
But there was no water,
And the croaking was fainter now . . .

WHERE WILL I BE?

One step, two steps, three steps, four,
Eight steps, nine steps, ten steps, more,
Wandering the paths through day and darkness,
Feeling the joys of movement:
Two days after yesterday,
Where will I be tomorrow?

Watching the sunset over Kilimanjaro,
White water rafting in Oregon,
Skiing in the Pyrenees,
Pleasing a mistress in Phuket,
Picking potatoes in a Cheshire field,
Where will I be tomorrow?

It is but a page away,
A glimpse over the shoulder of time,
Tantalisingly near, like the bouquet of wine
Trapped temporarily by the cork in the bottle,
But why, why, why do I ask,
Where will I be tomorrow?

TISSUE PAPER

Can we assume that in days gone by
Content was the *raison d'être*,
And wrappings and string were just the cover;
At best a protective layer,
Like cured skins of forest beast
Clad the loins of man?

When did adornment start,
Those illustrated coverings
Which boost the identity of that within;
Attractiveness, notoriety,
Like feathers in the cap of man
Or gaudy buttons on his suit?

When did wrappings dominate
And content lose significance,
Thrusting a one-dimensional overview
On all endeavour,
Like the true composition of modern man
Is in the clothes he wears?

FULLY ROBED

He stood at the door of the church
And asked for God to guide him,
The only scrap of symbolism he had
Was the clothes he wore,
For he was naked of soul.

He looked at the sun, the world outside,
And felt the empty church behind
With its half-open door,
He had not the wherewithal
To be fully a man of God,
And equally a man of the world.

But for good or ill
Is this not the fate of man;
A manipulation
Beyond his own understanding,
Free to roam his own environs
Until transformed?

Still he stood and stared
Across the graves to the public road,
His robes hanging loose about him.

CLOUDS

I have sent the clouds away
To where they belong;
The sun is out
And there is happiness.

Clouds have their place
In times of sadness,
Fear, doubt,
Terror, uncertainty.

But they shouldn't come
To darken unwary hearts,
On just a whim
And at their own volition.

Yet we seem to encourage them
When we pray
For forgiveness of sins,
About which we know nothing.

Yes, I have sent the clouds away,
Defeated them;
The sun is high
And there is happiness.

But for how long?

FAIRYLAND

If you ask me where it is
I will not respond;
I do not know.

It is improbable
That it is an emerging state
In darkest Africa.

Or an outback Australian town,
Where they turn kangaroo pelts
Into money belts.

But if you need to know,
Perhaps it's a semi in Solihull,
Where the Adamsons live.

But why 'fairyland'?
I don't know,
Ask them!

CLIMBING BACK

Sleight of hand or turn of key, whichever,
It takes a minute, only perhaps a moment,
But when, when, when will that moment be?

Bright colours instead of blackness,
And when the iron doors opened,
An air of dancing and of freedom.

Not wanting re-embodiment,
Only new feelings for an ancient hand,
And refreshment for a mind distressed.

Sleight of hand; heavy clouds have gone,
Fairy slippers replace leaden boots,
Gossamer wings where funereal drapes had hung.

HAPPINESS (2)

The notice on the door read,
Please knock and walk in,
I did knock and walked in,
The place was full of happiness.

It came from the ceiling and out from the walls
And up from the floor like shooting stars,
Thrusting aside and pushing out through the door
All contamination.

It became the only feeling,
All other emotion whose job it was
To provide some equilibrium
Was overcome and flung beyond reach.

Thus it was that concentrated happiness
Filled the space
Vacated by all else,
And soon became commonplace, the norm.

Then the room imploded
Through pressure from the world outside,
Bricks and mortar and ceiling fell,
And all humanity was stripped away.

If happiness ever comes again,
Let it be in thin slices, measured;
Like smoked salmon on crusty bread,
Tempered with a sip of fine champagne.

NATURE STUDY

Wind in the willows on the river bank,
Wild grasses growing in the hedge,
Deep in the forest at a quiet spot,
Generations of leaves congregating
Mould away, covering paths;
Silence and stillness in the midday sun.

And in the afternoon, full-bellied swans
Lazing about on the pond,
Fishes leaping for the sake of it,
Frogs in the reeds seeking coolness,
Deer, ears pricked, coming down to drink
Momentarily pause, then shy away.

If nature manifests into naturalness
What then can be more natural
Than a hungry baby crying,
Than a child enchanted by a toy shop window,
Than a parent seeking security,
Or an old man dying?

MAN IN A HURRY

He is the water in a waterfall,
Air in the balloon,
He is power,
The shock in the earthquake,
The rumble and fire of the volcano,
He is the man with a mission.

He comes to make a difference,
To alter things.
He knows no limit
And goes as quickly as he came.
The time he is here is infinitesimal,
The impression he leaves is lasting.

He comes; he changes everything,
Everywhere is rebuilt.
Any rubble left is to be brushed away.
Some people pretend he never happened,
Others ask what he is all about,
A few think he is the Messiah.

POETRY

What is poetry today?
It should reflect life and fantasy
In rhythm and rhyme,
Art and music,
Allegory;
And in defence of modern times,
Should perhaps be performed
With an economy of words.

It is complex, nevertheless,
As a painting is complex
With colours, with form and with brushwork;
It illuminates, it questions, it researches;
It goes back in time
And forward into eternity;
It doesn't start with birth
Or finish with death.

It has touches of teasing and mockery,
It illustrates simply, profound wisdoms,
Like the sound of rain
On trees in full leaf:
The reader is rewarded with new insight
Of familiar things,
With the opening up of vistas
Unrecognized before.

Or can the reader be side-tracked
Into muddy waters,
Or the green slime
Of intellectual snobbery;
Suffering poetry to be violated
When stupidity is made to seem wise,
The commonplace disguised by allegorical absurdity
That when unravelled
Falls apart?

It is hoped that time, sieving nonsense
From current fashion,
Will create true reflections of today,
With essays that will stretch imagination,
Pushing out the boundaries of contemporary poetry,
Putting it alongside that of yesteryear,
To stand proud, head held high
With confidence to face the new era.

THE SUNDOWNER

At last we can relax,
The sun stretching on the horizon
And me in a wicker chair,
Sharing a six-pack from the fridge.
The intimate silence tells
All that need be said.

THE ANT

I am an ant,
I come up through the fireplace
And there is something wrong.
You say I don't belong
And puff a cloud of powder
In my face and on my tongue.
I die within a day of being born.

In your terms
My day is a hundred years.
In that time I have suckled,
I have grown,
I have worked my being
To the bone,
I have copulated and ensured
The continuance of my race.

In my dying breath I ask,
Who are you,
What task have you performed
Commensurate with your size,
Your strength,
Your stretching out of life,
Your claim to knowledge,
Your superiority?

In the time that you have taken
My breed has been and done and gone
And come again a million times.

WORDS UNWRITTEN

Full moon buffeted by the icy wind
Throws silver shimmerings through the bare tree boughs,
And lights the familiar window from outside,
And aggravates the shadows, where one would think
No one would openly venture on such a night,
But someone does.

They do not see him from inside the room,
For the curtains are drawn, and their brave new world extends
Only to where their eyes can see and hold
The concept of the present immediacy;
Identical footprints of past generations obliterated
By youthful enthusiasm.

Another step along the moonlit road,
Another glimpse of understanding,
Add more complexity to the horizon's depth,
Sending it further back beyond his reach;
Behind, the illuminated window tempts
Him to return.

THE LONG ROAD

The speck at the end of the corridor
Is small and narrow,
And it is difficult to accept
That this is all that matters;
That the sides,
Above and all around,
Are nothing but a device
To focus the eyes.

To say that the one spot is light
And that light is the essence of life
Is an assumption I have been taught to accept.
But I find it hard
Because I am now not sure,
And my faith wavers.

What I do know
Is that I keep moving towards it,
Even shuffle and crawl;
I keep my eye on it at all times,
And sometimes
When my thoughts seem to be asleep
I look at it trance-like,
Fixed with a stubbornness,
Afraid that if I let go
It will be gone forever,
And there will be nothing.

What faith I have
Is questioned by this endless darkness,
Denigrating the present,
Favouring the future.
Within me there is revolt,
A desire for immediate illumination.
What I need, now,
Is heaven brought down to earth,
For the speck is aloof and distant.

I find it incomprehensible
That God chooses to make me so imperfect
That I struggle;
It is as if God Himself
Is unsure of what He has created.

What is there to stop me
Exploring those corridors of darkness,
Splitting them apart,
Widening the apertures,
Grasping today the aspirations of tomorrow,
Opening them up to one vast expanse?

The sun would rise and spread warmth;
The air would be clean and clear.
The trees would reach out over the fields,
And in the lake fishes would swim;
Why complicate life?

THE COUNTRY SUNDAY

I canna understand why them townies
Have flitted into next door,
It bein' damp an' all.
Ol' Ned couldna give it away
When 'e was alive,
Wot with its leaky slates
An' them wotsit woodworm things.

Now scaffolding's up an' new winders
And a alaminium gree'ouse
The likes o'what 'ave never bin seen
In these parts afore.

The place is dead,
Except for 'Enery goin' church
In 'is granddad's suit,
And there's nothing else but crisp bags flippin' about
And cinders steamin' 'ot, 'issing like
When I've just chucked 'em,
To fill up the 'ole inth' road.

At the back
Dora's old pram with no wheels
Is stuck inth' ditch,
Where the slutchy path runs down
To the duck pond that was,
Now full of rusty bike frames
And broke motor car bits;
As I sez, everythin's dead 'ereabouts.

But I forgit
It's Sunday!
Tomorrer there'll be washin' out,
Jem'll be spraying somebody's car;
Kids with their arse-ends out
Will be chuckin' brickends at the street lamp
And kickin' beer cans about;
Maud will be tryin' to start up her Mini
And find 'er tyres flat.
She'll be creatin'
An' livenin' things up a bit.

Yea, this is more like it,
The townies 'll settle in all reet,
I wonder if they'll want their allotment
Or could I let it out to our Joe
Quiet like
And make a bob or two.
Twud be a pity to let all that rotted cowmuck
Go to waste.

CRANAGE VILLAS

Childhood visits to my aunt
Were always on a Sunday;
Neglected homework
Vied with the call of the outdoors.

To learn verbatim
Psalm 121 from the Bible,
Jostled with the sounds of bird song
And the rustle of wind in the trees.

The agony, the irony
That Sundays and the Word of God
Should destroy my communications with His other beings
Still lies deep within me.

I never went into the woods
After I left school,
Or walked again in the meadow
Knee-deep in grass and wild flowers.

I forsook the sand martin
Burrowing deep into the river bank,
And the skylark like a dot in the sky
Rising in full song.

As I travel now that country lane
I still hear the falterings of Psalm 121,
Obliterating the thoughts
That should have filled those Sunday afternoons.

NIL QUANTUM EST

The last of the July daylight
Trickles away into the cracked earth;
Nothing replaces it,
No velvet cushions or intrigues.
What a misconception
That coming darkness is a comfort in waiting!

The night passes into weeks, into years;
No impetus, no promise, even
No thought of a new perspective.
The long silence stretches out
Across the playing fields,
And the darkness is forever.

TRAINS

Speed adds surface dimension to passing of time
And quick escape from accountability:
The slow train allows for wisdom at every stop,
To consolidate the progression forward step by step.

YOUTH

Body and mind combined,
Waiting to react
To all about it that is new;
But frightened with its unfamiliarity
Retreats
Or advances in such a way
As to show its immaturity.

Body and mind
Unformed, uninformed,
Not having elected to exist:
Is there any wonder it cannot tell
Whether this be heaven or hell.

THE FLOW

Make it simple as you would for a child,
Slow, interacting
One part with another,
Make it smooth as night comes into day,
And years pile upon years,
As leaves come and then fall,
As eggs hatch into birds and grow –
No jerks or gaps or misunderstandings.
Let there be no sudden hiccup
Or change of pace.

Whoosh!
It comes, a great wallop
Incongruous, indigestible,
A rock rising unexpected
From the flat field of wheat,
Thunderstorm turning daylight into night
Shaking the foundation
And the planned ways of things,
River rising above its banks.

But keep it simple as you would for a child,
Smooth the tidal wave
Till it ripples and stems
And is absorbed into the whole pattern,
Helping carry forward
Those clean, clear, natural lines,
Now a little more enlightened
Than they were before the portent
Of the rude interruption:
Make it simple as you would for a child.

WAITING

I ask:
"Are we waiting for something?"
Isn't this an idle question
For doesn't waiting imply
That there is some expectation?

But if the reply is:
"We are not waiting for anything.
We are just waiting . . ."
Is this then a void situation?
But if it exists
It cannot be void
For even nothing is something.

In this circumstance, is waiting a delusion,
An easement,
An escapism?
Is it sometimes a defining moment,
A moment of quiet truth
That stands tall in itself
And needs no support
Or explanation?

INSPIRATION

Comes a moment,
Unexpected from foreign field,
That highlights the problem and the solution,
Sorts out the ignominy from the glory,
The symmetry from the confusion,
And overwhelmingly displays
The compatibility
Of things so seemingly contradictory.

It is a moment
That catches one unawares
And is soon gone,
Leaving a ball of fire
To glow in the dark.

THE WOODMAN'S HUT

Rain falls on field flat and monotonous,
But dances in the trees
And pricks the pond
Into circular commotion.

It pelts like nails into the leaky roof,
And runs in miniature rivers
Through the broken doorway,
Into the dry dust.

The close incessant rain
Brings chill excitement,
A pitting against the elements;
Sensuous feelings
That would get lost in city streets.

STUDY IN SCARLET

Deep country winter
Reduces the world
To closed doors,
To a book by Conan Doyle.

Fantasies of gas light and a coal fire
Flick shadows across the gloom,
The crêpe de Chine,
The ruby glass,
The mirror, the chiffonier;
Thick fumes from Holmes' pipe
Add atmosphere.

Outside, the mists
Of London streets and alleyways;
The cobblestones, the hansom cab,
All shrouded in clinging damp
That frames
The urchin holding tight
The horse's rein.

Suddenly the illusion is gone,
The Victorian scene tossed
Into oblivion
By yelping hounds
And horses churning up the lawn;
Pandemonium,
As the fox breaks cover
And the seething mass
Swarms down the bank
To the brook,
And is gone.

All that is left
Is the gentle waft of silence
And the ruined lawn;
Silt settles in deep pools
As the brook recovers its equilibrium;
A piece of stone terracing has disappeared
And the remains of a wild primrose.

From the last of the riders
An arrogant apology;
The hunt insurance
Will cover the damage.
A crack of the whip
And he too is gone,
Vanished
Like the rooms in Baker Street.

The door shuts.
Again deep country winter
Reduces the world
To a room,
To central heating,
But outside a wretched howl
Reverberates
In the bare trees.

CONSCIENCE

I do not know you,
I do not know who you are,
I will not stoop
To acknowledge your existence
By asking from where you came,
Or what is your business.
You are invisible.
And although I accept invisibility
As a manifest building block
You hide your non-existence
Under its guise.
You are not even a trick of imagination,
And yet …

And yet, there is a presence holding me back,
An electric shock, paralysis that strikes
Not just my limbs
Which uncontrollably flap about
But my thoughts too have stopped,
Then turned back along the narrow path
To yesterday, to the cringing deed
That performs again and will not go away.
Even in bed in the quiet of the night
My soul lifts up and quivers, and shrinks
To a size embracing only the past.
The future a perpetual vacuum,
A simple nothingness.

I am a fool, the witless one,
Who thought a stroke of whitewash
Would expurgate the stain,
And leave not only innocence
But open the gateway to treasures
That lie by streams and waterfalls,
And to praise and fame unsolicited.
Or can it be
That you mistakenly appeared,
And by sleight of hand can be manoeuvred away.
I am tired now;
Allow me to sleep and dream.
Will tomorrow be another day?

THE SHED

I have built me a shed.
I expect, like you,
To go on living until I am dead,
And when I am dead
Bury me please in the shed,
And shed
No tears,
Thinking that I am dead,
For I will go on living,
Living in that shed.

CROSSROADS

Reach for the door,
Open it,
And through the darkness
There is light.

Leave it shut,
And the remaining present
Commits one
To the leftover uncomfortable bits.

Which way;
On towards the newness,
Avoiding the boring detail
Of the present?

Or turn inwards
To dominant concentration,
Risking overpolish
To oblivion?

EGO

Of them all, you are the best,
You leave behind you all the rest;
You are the sunshine in the stars,
You are the cream in Milky Bars.

But when you are gone
And I have become the one,
You will have joined the rest
And I will be the best.

PRISONER

As he is released,
A new sky
Extends above the prison gate,
And grows in bold configuration.

So dominant is it
That the effluent from the past
Trickles out of the cobbled yard
And sticks unnoticed to his feet.

Too late, he reaches for the sky;
The taxi door slams
And he is whisked away
Back into the dark underworld.

GAME PLAN

There is a blackbird in the tree
With a squirming worm;
That he is interested in me
Is a fallacy
For she is there in another tree
Knowing that in the nest her family waits
Impatiently.

"Why don't you go away?" she chirps
Trying to distract me,
Whilst he flaps
Nonchalantly unconcerned
And wings away elsewhere,
Ostensibly.

"Little do you know," I want to whisper,
"That in your various absences
I have counted your eggs
And seen them hatch,
And I would be the last
To cause alarm
Or do any harm,
Wilfully."

But she would not understand
And quietly I move away
From this field of play,
Caringly.

CONSEQUENCE

When darkness fights
The wherewithal of light,
Shadows
Shaped by filigreed artistic hands
Play animations on the wall.

When white frost melts
To meet the feeble sun,
Icicles elongate
And run
In liquid diamonds.

When winter clouds break
And ease
Into beginnings of spring,
There comes the blossom on trees,
And bees.

When sperms ejaculate
From their confines to explore,
They discover foreign genes,
And beget
A new creation.

SILENCE

It hangs like dust in shafts of light
That comes from high-up window panes,
It creeps from corners to fill the space
Left by harmony, discord, sorrow and joy.

It is sensed in the memorial plaque
Cared for on the painted wall,
And felt in the cool unfettered air,
When outside it is grumpily hot.

It is enhanced by the solitary pair
Of hobnailed boots traversing the aisle,
Echoing in the raftered roof
And by the toll of the single bell.

WHY

Why do we grow up
Instead of growing down,
When after all we do end up
Six feet underground?

WORKS BUS 1956

Lowry figures,
Beneath early morning street lamps,
Huddle together.

Muffled faces
Tucked in winter coats,
Scarves and hats.

Icy winds
Slice round corners,
Like carving knives.

Ancient bus
Sucking up its load,
Roars off.

Tail lights flicker,
Gears grind,
Smoke pours out.

The street,
Now empty,
But for the cold.